THE CHANGING FACE OF
INDIA

Text by David Cumming
Photography by Chris Fairclough

RAINTREE
STECK-VAUGHN
PUBLISHERS

A Harcourt Company

Austin   New York
www.raintreesteckvaughn.com

Published by Raintree Steck-Vaughn Publishers, an imprint of Steck-Vaughn Company

Library of Congress Cataloging-in-Publication Data is available upon request.

ISBN 0-7398-4966-2

Printed in Italy. Bound in the United States.

1 2 3 4 5 6 7 8 9 0 LB 06 05 04 03 02

Acknowledgments

The publishers would like to thank the following for their contributions to this book: Chris Fairclough—interview research; Rob Bowden—statistical research; Nick Hawkin—illustrations on pages 6, 22, 24, 27, 33, 36, 38; Peter Bull—map on page 8. All photographs are by Chris Fairclough except: Impact/Caroline Penn 37 (top); Panos 13; Popperfoto 10; Steve White-Thomson 9 (lower).

Consultant: Dr. Tony Binns, University of Sussex

Contents

1 "Silicon City"

In 1537 a powerful warlord named Kempe Gowda watched his followers build a new city in southern India. A prophet brought him a dish of boiled beans to eat and foretold that the city would have a great future. Thinking that the beans were lucky, Kempe Gowda named the city after them— Bengaluru. Today it is called Bangalore, and it is thriving not on beans, but on silicon chips.

Bangalore is the fifth-largest city in India and one of the fastest-growing in Asia. It is at the heart of the "Electronic Revolution" presently sweeping across India. It is full of colleges for learning about computers and factories for assembling them. Offices are busy with software programmers.

▲ *These people are working as guides at one of the regular IT exhibitions in Bangalore. Firms from India and abroad attend them to get more clients.*

▼ *At home and at work, the people of Bangalore are benefiting from improved communications, such as satellite links.*

Using satellite links, experts in Bangalore can work on computer problems affecting companies in Europe and the United States. Since India is several hours ahead of Europe and the United States, this type of work can be carried out overnight, without causing disruption to the foreign companies' businesses.

These developments have resulted in a lot of money flowing into Bangalore. Its citizens now have one of the highest standards of living in India. The latest fashions and fast foods are on sale in the new shopping malls. High-rise blocks of apartments have sprung up, equipped with everything from cable TV to fitness centers.

The prophet certainly proved correct in her predicitons—Bangalore is booming.

▶ Advertising billboards have sprung up all over Bangalore, promoting the city's booming businesses.

INDIA: KEY FACTS

Area: 1,269,340 square miles (3,288,000 sq km)

Population: 846 million (1991 census); current estimate = 1 billion

Population density: 99 persons per sq mile (256 persons per sq km)

Capital city: New Delhi (9 million)

Other main cities: Mumbai (formerly Bombay; 13 million), Calcutta (11 million), Chennai (formerly Madras; 4 million), Bangalore (3.5 million), Hyderabad (3 million)

Highest mountain: Kanchenjunga 28,210 feet (8,598 m)

Longest river: Brahmaputra 1,763 miles (2,840 km)

Main languages: Hindi, English, and 13 regional languages

Major religions: Hinduism (82% of people), Islam (12%), Christianity (2%), Sikhism (2%), Others (2%)

Money: Rupee (100 paise = 1 rupee)

2 Past Times

In 1947 India gained its independence after centuries of British rule. Finally, India had the freedom to prosper for its own people. Under British rule, India was used for growing raw materials such as cotton and *jute* which was then taken for Great Britain's economic gain.

The Indian government "closed its doors" to the rest of the world to give its new industries time to develop. Foreign firms were prevented from setting up in the country. Firms that wanted to sell their goods in India had to pay high taxes in order to do so, thus making their products very expensive in comparison with those produced in India.

In the 1980s, Indian businesses started to question the "closed door" idea. True, it had helped them to get started, but they now lagged behind those abroad. The government had no option but to seek outside help to catch up. In the 1990s it reluctantly opened India's doors to foreign companies and lowered the barriers to trade.

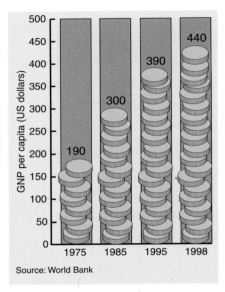

Source: World Bank

▲ *Since 1975, the amount of money India earns from the goods it produces has increased rapidly.*

IN THEIR OWN WORDS

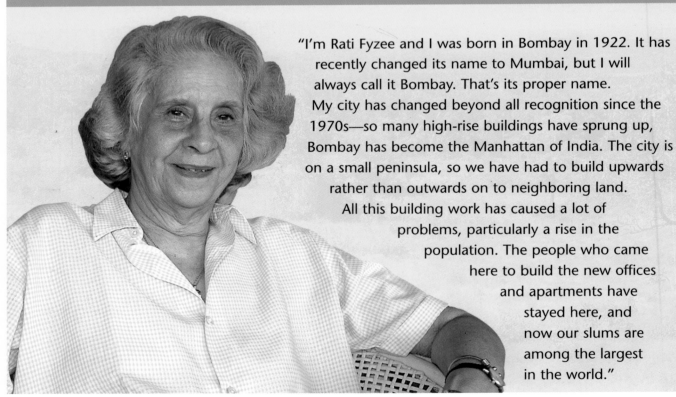

"I'm Rati Fyzee and I was born in Bombay in 1922. It has recently changed its name to Mumbai, but I will always call it Bombay. That's its proper name.

My city has changed beyond all recognition since the 1970s—so many high-rise buildings have sprung up, Bombay has become the Manhattan of India. The city is on a small peninsula, so we have had to build upwards rather than outwards on to neighboring land.

All this building work has caused a lot of problems, particularly a rise in the population. The people who came here to build the new offices and apartments have stayed here, and now our slums are among the largest in the world."

6

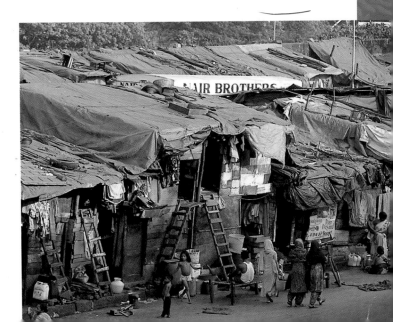

Money and up-to-date technology poured into India's businesses. New factories were built, equipped with the latest machinery. Modern ways of working were introduced.

Overall, this "shake-up" has benefited India. Millions have never had it so good. They have plenty of work and plenty of money in their wallets. The shops are full of goods for them to buy. However, there are still millions of other Indians who have yet to notice any change in their lives.

▲ *Mumbai has benefited greatly from improved trade with businesses all over the globe.*

▶ *Millions of people have been attracted to Mumbai in the hope of a better life. Sadly, housing is limited and many of them end up in slums like this one.*

3 Landscape and Climate

From space, India looks like a small triangle sticking out of the gigantic continent of Asia. However, it is nearly 1,274,000 square miles (3,300,000 sq km) in size: about 1,988 miles (3,200 km) long and 1,678 miles (2,700 km) at its widest point. This makes India the seventh-largest country in the world.

▼ *This map shows the main features of India's landscape and major cities. The main towns and regions mentioned in this book are also shown.*

Different Landscapes

India has a great variety of landscapes, including chilly snow-covered mountains, a hot, dusty desert, and thick forests. It can be divided up into three regions.

The first region contains the world's highest mountain range, the Himalayas. They extend across the north of India and contain Kanchenjunga. At 28,210 feet (8,598 m), it is the highest point in India and the third-highest mountain in the world.

The Ganges River occupies the second region. The flat, open land in the Ganges valley stretches across the middle of India and the soils in this area are good for farming. The Thar Desert runs along the western edge of the region; little can grow here.

The final region is the Deccan. This is a high plateau which takes up much of south India. Two ranges of forested hills, the Western Ghats and Eastern Ghats, lie on either side of it, separating it from the Indian Ocean.

▼ *Leh is a town in Ladakh, high in the Himalaya Mountains of northwest India.*

▲ *The palm-fringed beaches of Goa are popular with Indian vacationers, as well as with foreign tourists.*

The Importance of the Monsoon

India's climate is split into three seasons: cool, hot, and wet. The cool season lasts from October through February. Then the hot season begins and lasts throughout May. Temperatures often reach 81°F (45°C) in the Thar Desert. The wet season begins in June, when a wind called the monsoon blows in from the Indian Ocean. It usually ends in September.

▲ These trees and houses were destroyed by the cyclone that hit the eastern state of Orissa in 1999.

▼ Little grows in Rajasthan's Thar Desert, except scrub for these sheep to nibble.

The monsoon normally brings much-needed rain for farmers' thirsty crops. In some years, though, there is little rain; in other years, too much. Either way, the consequences can be devastating: ruined harvests or drowned villages.

The monsoon frequently stirs up fierce storms, called cyclones, in the Bay of Bengal. Their winds create towering tidal waves, which hammer the east coast at the end of the wet season, causing enormous damage.

Climate Change

India's weather is becoming unpredictable and more extreme. In May 1998 record-breaking temperatures of 120°F (49°C) in the north caused 3,000 deaths. In September 1999, an unusually strong cyclone killed 10,000 people and left an estimated 7.5 million homeless. In August 2000, while the northwest was suffering from the worst drought in over a century, the northeast was experiencing serious flooding. Over 850 people lost their lives and 16 million were forced to flee to safety on high ground. Many weather scientists believe the climate is changing as a result of global warming and fear similar disasters in the future.

IN THEIR OWN WORDS

"My name is Saturam Bidha. We are very poor farmers and we live on the edge of the Thar Desert in Rajasthan. We own four acres of land. We grow a few vegetables and some fodder for our three goats, which we use for milk. We can grow just enough food for ourselves. There's little left over to sell at the market, so we rarely have any money to spend.

"There has been no rain in this part of Rajasthan for the past seven years. That has made it very difficult for our plants to grow and we have had to cut down on the amount we eat at meals. Even the goats have suffered. They have produced less milk because we haven't been able to feed them properly."

Natural Resources

4

Minerals

The most important mineral resources found in India are iron ore and coal. India is one of the world's biggest producers of iron ore. Deposits of iron ore are found all over the country, but the largest mines are in the eastern states of Bihar and Orissa.

IN THEIR OWN WORDS

"I am Kalid Mohammed. I'm 35 years old and I live in Jaipur, where I work cutting and polishing precious stones. It is a job which requires great skill and it took me nearly two years to learn. Jaipur is famous for the red garnet and rhodolite stones found in the desert nearby. I also work on emeralds and rubies from Brazil and Zambia.

"The stones are sent to jewelers in Japan, Singapore, and Hong Kong when we have finished cutting and polishing them. There are three of us in this workshop and each year we work on stones worth over $1 million. We are part of an important export industry in India. It's also an important industry in Jaipur. More and more tourists visit this area now and many of them like to buy a gemstone as a special vacation souvenir."

IN THEIR OWN WORDS

"I'm Vinay Goyal and I'm a production manager at my father's factory, where we make brass and copper products. Here in Moradabad there are 11,000 companies involved in this type of work. My father started our business with $200, 30 years ago, and now we are one of the largest companies—we employ 200 men full-time and up to 700 part-time workers. Most of these men come from local villages and when they're not working for us they are subsistence farmers. Our products are exported all over the world, and much of it goes to the United States and Europe. Our profit is in excess of $4 million per year. Moradabad has always been famous for brass and copper, but in recent years we've expanded into stainless steel and iron in order to attract a broader range of customers."

India's coal reserves are the fourth largest in the world. They contain enough to meet the country's needs until well into the next century. Bauxite (used for making aluminum), copper, and manganese ores are the other major minerals. There are also smaller quantities of chromite, zinc, gold, silver, and diamonds.

▶ *These miners in Bihar are preparing dynamite, which they use to blast away the surface of the rock.*

Energy Sources

About 80 percent of India's electricity is generated in coal-fired power plants. Another 17 percent is produced by hydroelectric power. A tiny amount is generated using wind and solar power and the rest comes from nuclear power plants. Many people are opposed to the development of hydroelectric power plants because vast areas of land have to be flooded to create reservoirs. India will rely more on nuclear power than on hydroelectric power in the future.

The main oilfields are in the northeast and under the Indian Ocean, off Mumbai (Bombay). After refining, oil from these reserves provides about 30 percent of India's needs. Natural gas is also produced in the offshore oilfields. Most of it is used to make chemical fertilizers.

▲ *This woman is preparing animal dung for use as a fuel for cooking—a good example of natural recycling which the government is encouraging in rural areas.*

Electricity Shortages

Although India now generates nearly twenty times as much electricity as it did at Independence in 1947, it is not enough. The demand for electricity is much greater, and this is not simply because cities and industries have grown. Now, millions of villagers have access to electricity whereas in 1947, only one half of 1 percent of all villages were connected to the National Grid. Today it is 75 percent. The shortage of electricity is most noticeable during the hot season, when air conditioners and fans are working at full blast in the cities. Power outages lasting several hours are part of daily life.

▶ *This overloaded electricity pole illustrates the great demand for power in India.*

IN THEIR OWN WORDS

"My name is Suraj. I'm 12 years old and I live in the capital city of New Delhi. We live in a block of apartments with one hundred other families. During the summer it gets very hot and there are always power outages, because everyone has their air conditioners and fans on full blast. We have a huge diesel generator that provides electricity when there is a power outage but the trouble is, it often breaks down. Then I miss my favorite TV shows. My mother says it's a good opportunity to do my homework—by candlelight!

"At school we have been learning about alternative power, such as solar energy. We have so much sunshine in India that I think in the future the government should use it to provide more electricity."

Basic Needs

Food Sources

India is lucky because 51 percent of its land can be used for growing crops. Few other countries have such a large amount of land available for food production. The main crops grown by farmers are sugarcane, rice, vegetables, wheat, and fruit.

India is also fortunate in having 4,350 miles (7,000 km) of coastline, which means that the surrounding seas can be fished for food. Pomfret (a small flat fish), kingfish, and mackerel are caught in large numbers. In recent years fleets of large trawlers (big net, commercial fishermen) have been criticized for catching too much fish. Now local fishermen complain that their nets are never full.

Revolutions in Farming

Until the 1970s India's farmers could not grow enough to feed the quickly growing population and food had to be bought from abroad. Then the use of new types of seed increased the size of the harvests. This "Green Revolution" meant that India

▲ *These villagers have been night-fishing just off the beach.*

IN THEIR OWN WORDS

"I'm Yashwant Anant Tandal and I'm a fisherman based in Mumbai. I started fishing when I was 17, like my father and grandfather before me. I have two sons, but they don't want to be fishermen. They say it's too much hard work and they'd rather work in an air-conditioned office. The big factory ships catch tons of fish and are killing off the small fishermen like me. In 1999, thousands of us went to Delhi to protest outside parliament. We are still waiting to see if the government will help us."

had food to spare. The problem was that the seeds needed a lot of expensive chemical fertilizers and pesticides to make them grow well. So only rich farmers could afford to plant them. Poor farmers had to borrow money to buy the seeds but if their harvests failed—as a result of bad weather, for example—they could not afford to repay the money they had borrowed. As a result of this, many people lost their farms.

Now another farming revolution is causing concern. This is the introduction of genetically modified (GM) seeds—seeds that have been adapted to make them produce bigger harvests, or to make them resistant to disease. Once again, these seeds will be expensive. Another problem with the Green Revolution was that the chemicals used harmed the environment. No one is sure how GM seeds will affect the environment. Many Indian farmers want further tests to be carried out before they decide whether to use them.

▲ *The warm, wet climate of southern India is ideal for growing rice. Here, water buffalo are grazing in the rice paddies.*

5 The Changing Environment

The natural environment is very important in India because 73 percent of the population relies on it for work and for its daily needs. These are the people who live outside the towns and cities in the 580,000 villages.

The forests surrounding the homes in the countryside supply wood. The land is used for growing food and for grazing. Nearby rivers and ponds provide water for washing and drinking. Animals supply milk and a means of transportation. Animal dung is used as a fertilizer and as a fuel. Local herbs and plants are a source of medicines.

The environment is also important to India's industries. Nearly 50 percent of the goods produced every year are made from natural products, such as cotton for clothes and trees for paper or furniture. In view of its importance, you would expect that India would take better care of its environment. However, this has not always been the case.

▼ *Cows are a common sight in towns and cities. They eat some of the waste that lies in the streets but they cannot eat the plastic garbage that is becoming more and more common.*

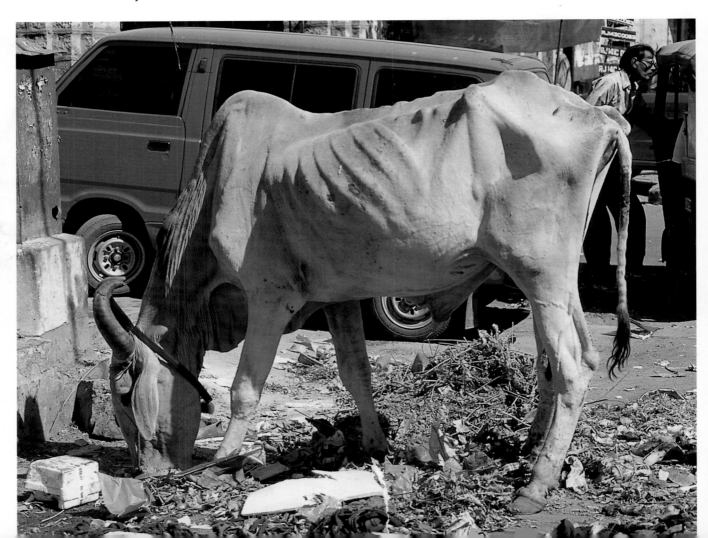

IN THEIR OWN WORDS

"My name is Manish Gupta. I'm 22 and I live in Agra. We're proud to have one of the most famous buildings in the world—the Taj Mahal. It took 22 years to complete, from 1630 to 1652. When it was first built, the marble was pure white. Now pollution in the air is turning it a dirty yellow color.

"Fortunately, the government is so concerned that it has passed a law to reduce the smog. There is a 12-mile (20-km) smoke-free zone around Agra. All the old 'smokestack' factories have had to move outside this zone. It has been expensive to do this, but it will protect our wonderful Taj Mahal and tourists will still come to see it."

Environmental Damage

Cities and industries have created a lot of pollution. This has been pumped into the air in the form of poisonous fumes from vehicle exhausts and factory chimneys. Factories have dumped harmful chemicals into the rivers. These have joined the raw sewage already there because the cities do not have the facilities to treat it. The filthy water kills fish and the unsuspecting villagers who must use it for drinking.

▲ *India's cities are now so full that many families are forced to live among the waste that has been washed down the rivers.*

Disappearing Forests

Every year 1.5 million acres of forests are chopped down in India. Both villagers and industries are to blame for this.

Villagers need the wood for fuel and for constructing new homes. As village populations have increased, so has the demand for wood. Now villagers spend a large part of each day searching for wood because they have to travel further to find it.

Industries use wood as a fuel. As they have expanded, they have used up more and more trees. Some industries, such as the paper industry, use wood for fuel and for making their products, so they need even more of it. Other industries need

IN THEIR OWN WORDS

"I'm Rajesh Kumar. I'm 21 and I've been working as a carpenter for seven years. I was lucky and went to college to study carpentry for two days a week. There's a lot of new building work in Agra and carpenters are in demand. Although I learned the traditional methods of carpentry, using hand tools that I made myself, we're now so busy that I use some power tools. These are very expensive and difficult to fix if they break. Most of the timber we use is grown in India but recently we have started to import some soft wood from Australia and New Zealand."

the land occupied by forests. For example, forests have been cut down to increase the land available for tea and rubber plantations. Forests have also had to make way for larger coal and iron-ore mines.

In the countryside, valuable soil has been lost because of deforestation. Without trees' roots to hold the soil together, and their leaves to shelter it from the monsoon, soil is carried away by the wind and rain. The land then becomes useless for agriculture. Forests also play a part in the water cycle. Rivers and underground reservoirs may dry up when they have gone.

▶ *This area of lush green forest is in a national park in southern India, where it is protected from farmers greedy for the land, and from industries that want to use the timber.*

▼ *Farmers in dry areas like Rajasthan are badly affected by the soil erosion and disruption to water supplies that can result from the loss of tree cover.*

The growth of India's cities has also contributed to the loss of forests. In 1961, 18 percent of India's people lived in cities. Today, the figure is 29 percent (which is a figure equal to the entire population of India in 1941). The population of Calcutta, the second-biggest city, doubled between 1960 and 2000 to 12 million.

Extra people means extra electricity. To meet the needs of Mumbai and Delhi, a hydroelectric power plant with a massive dam is being built on the river Narmada. When it is completed, 350,000 acres of forest will be drowned.

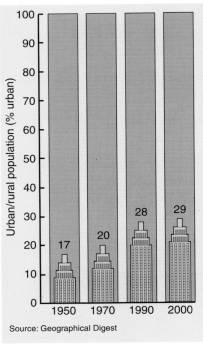

▲ *Since 1950, towns and cities have grown rapidly.*

◀ *The growth in car ownership is one of the main reasons for the increased pollution in Mumbai.*

Tackling the Problems

Today there is more awareness in India of the need to look after the environment. In the cities, new laws are reducing vehicle and factory emissions. In the countryside, the government is supporting the replanting of forests. It is also encouraging the use of alternative fuels, such as solar power and biogas (methane gas produced from rotting animal dung). Many conservation parks have been set up in which humans are forbidden to live or work. These protect the trees and plants as well as safeguarding the wildlife. Lions and tigers, for example, once existed in large numbers. The shrinking forests made them easier to hunt, to the point where they were in danger of dying out. Indians hope that the parks are going to prevent this from happening.

▲ *This photo, taken in mid-afternoon, shows the smog hanging over New Delhi.*

IN THEIR OWN WORDS

"Hi, we're Megha, Vritika, Vani, and Shaloka. We all live in Delhi and we come to school by bus. Pollution is a big problem in Delhi and all the buses' diesel fumes make it worse. In 1999 the city authorities decided that all buses should run on cleaner CNG (which stands for Compressed Nitrogen Gas). They also banned buses over eight years old. Their engines discharged dirty, black smoke.

"Already the air is noticeably cleaner. We don't want all the exhaust pollution that we had in the past. We want a clean, green city. And we're going to make sure it happens. Things will be even better after the new metro system has been built."

6 The Changing Population

Living Longer

Since its independence in 1947, India's population has grown to just over 1 billion. It will soon overtake China to become the most populated nation in the world.

This is good news, because it shows that Indians are surviving longer. In 1947 an Indian could expect to live for only 32 years, and many babies died young. Huge improvements in health care and diet since then have resulted in life expectancy nearly doubling, to 63 years. More babies are also reaching adulthood now.

Population Growth

The bad news is that the size of families has not been reduced. More and more babies are growing into adults at the same time as more and more adults are reaching old age. Thus, the population has rocketed. About 16 million new Indians are born each year.

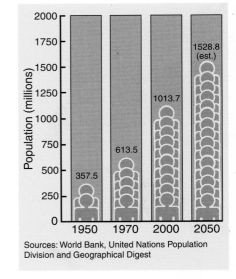

Sources: World Bank, United Nations Population Division and Geographical Digest

▲ *India's population has soared to over 1 billion.*

▼ *High-rise living in New Delhi, but not in a skyscraper. The poor in India's crowded cities have to make their homes wherever they can.*

IN THEIR OWN WORDS

"My name is Vineet Garg and I'm a doctor. I have had a private practice in the city of Moradabad for ten years. Most of my patients have money, but I have to look after the poor, too. Although treatment is free at the local government hospital, it is not very good. I charge poor people less than my richer patients.

"The growth of our population has caused many problems but thankfully two children per family will soon be the average, especially in the cities. Here the well-educated are having fewer children—two are enough for them."

Looking after all its people has become a near-impossible task for India, even though it is much wealthier than at the time of their independence. It has millions of poor people and, sadly, poverty makes the population problem worse. Poor parents want large families because their children can be sent out to work. They also want their children to look after them in their old age. Even though health care has improved, many babies still die young. So parents want many children to be sure that several of them will reach adulthood. For this reason, all attempts by the government to limit the size of families have failed among the poor. In the villages, home to most of India's poorest people, having four children is common.

▶ *A family in Bangalore crowded onto a motor bike. This has become a common sight in India's cities.*

Better Education

At Independence the government realized that India would only progress if its people were better educated. At that time only 15 percent of adults could read and write. Many new schools have been opened since then, and 52 percent of adults are now literate. However, this figure hides the fact that better educational provisions have not been spread evenly around the country. In the state of Kerala, 90 percent of adults are literate, but in Bihar the number drops to 38 percent.

Similarly, more money has been spent to provide education in cities than in villages. Most village schools are very basic. Equipment such as computers and even textbooks are unaffordable luxuries. Many village children still learn to write on slates, in the shade of a tree.

▲ *An expensive school for boys and girls in New Delhi. Wealthy parents apply for places at this school before their children are even born.*

IN THEIR OWN WORDS

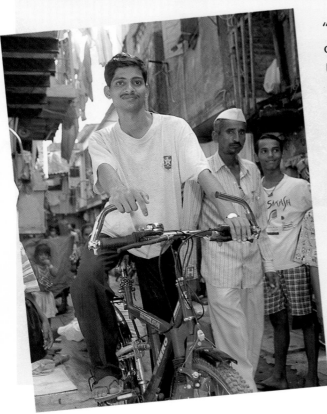

"I'm Prashant Vengurlekar. I'm in my second year of studying electronic engineering at Mumbai University. I come from a very poor family who could not afford to send me to college. Luckily, I won a scholarship because my exam results were so good and because I'm from the Vaishya caste of traders. [Turn to page 30 to find out more about the caste system.] Every year each caste is allocated a certain number of university spots. This ensures that poor people in India are given a chance to improve themselves.

"After college I want to work for the government. I want a job that I can use to help people like myself to get ahead in life. I've been helped. Now it's my turn to help others."

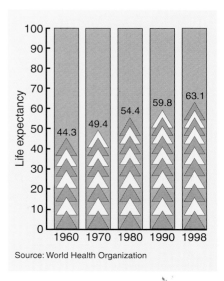

Improving Health Care

Many people have grown up in India without a proper education. This failure is one of the reasons behind India's low standards of health. The poor, especially, know little about good hygiene and the importance of a balanced diet. As a result, illnesses are common and spread rapidly. The government is trying to improve the situation by sending trained health workers into villages and into the slum areas of cities.

Social workers are being used to set up women's groups. This way, the government hopes that women will be given the confidence and knowledge to play a bigger part in their own families' and communities' futures. Studies all over the world show that this type of "empowering" of women helps greatly to lower family sizes, thereby slowing down India's rapidly growing population.

▲ *Life expectancy in India is increasing but it is still lower than that of many Western countries.*

▼ *It's not easy keeping clean in a poor home, but families do their best with what is available.*

7

Changes at Home

There has always been a difference between the way of life in India's cities and life in the villages. Since the 1990s the differences have become much more noticeable. The new India can be seen in the cities, the old one in the villages.

▲ *Three generations of this family share a home in Agra, Uttar Pradesh.*

Traditional Family Life

Indians believe that it is easier to survive life's hardships within a group than on your own. They like extended families, in which several generations live together under one roof. After getting married, a bride is expected to move in with her husband's family. From a young age children are taught to respect their elders. Throughout life they consult them before making a decision and their advice will be followed without question.

Arranged Marriages

Choosing a husband or wife for their children used to be one of the most important decisions taken by family elders. Today, arranged marriages are encouraged but no longer enforced. Families merely introduce youngsters and no

IN THEIR OWN WORDS

"My name is Pradnya and I'm 17. I've been talking to my parents about getting married. They have been very understanding. They want to be involved in finding me a suitable husband. However, they have made it clear that the final decision will be mine. Many of my friends are not so lucky. Their parents plan to decide everything. All my parents want me to do is marry a Hindu and then be happy and have children. But no more than two! There are already too many people in India. You try getting on the buses—impossible!"

demands are made of them. The tradition is changing. A growing number of young Indian men and women are making their own decisions about who to date and marry.

▲ *These worshippers are celebrating Diwali, the festival of lights, in a Hindu temple in Vrindavan.*

Religion

Religion is important to Indians. There are many religions in India, but the most important one is Hinduism. It is followed by 82 percent of the population. Most Hindu homes have a small shrine at which the family worships every day. They also pray regularly at a nearby temple and go on pilgrimages to holy places.

▶ *Damodar Das is a pupil at the Hari Krishna school in Vrindavan. Born in Nepal, he was sent to the school when he was eight to learn about the Hindu faith. There, his name was changed to Das, which means "servant of Krishna."*

Caste

For centuries Hindu society has been split into four groups, called castes, depending on people's lifestyles. At the top are *brahmins* (the priests). Next come *kshatriyas* (the soldiers and nobility), followed by the *vaishyas* (the businesspeople). Finally, there are *sudras* (the servants and craftspeople). Outside this system are the people who were once called the "untouchables" because they did the dirtiest jobs. They were renamed *harijans* (meaning "children of God") and are now referred to as the "scheduled castes."

Throughout the world, people generally marry within their own faith, and Hindus usually marry people of the same caste.

Challenges from Abroad

Traditional ways of behaving are undergoing the greatest change in the cities. Young city people, in particular, have

▼ *Traditionally, young couples were not allowed to meet alone before marriage, but things have changed in recent years.*

CLOSE-UP

"I am Padmanabh Goshwami and I am the priest of a Hindu temple. Fourteen generations of my family have been priests here, and my eldest son has been training all his life to take over from me.

"Needless to say, Hinduism is very important to me and my family. We are all worried that the foreign TV programs are damaging the Hindu religion and Indian society. You only have to look at how young people behave in Europe and America to realize how bad things could be in India.

"If our children turn away from Hinduism, everyone in India will be harmed. Hinduism teaches us to behave with respect to each other. Without that respect, mistrust will increase, and with it, crime and violence."

been influenced by contact with other cultures. This contact has come in many forms: from satellite TV and the opening of foreign shops and restaurants, to the arrival of tourists and businesspeople from abroad.

Some of the young people have started questioning age-old family values and customs. They would like the freedom that is given to foreigners of the same age. For example, they want to be free to wear Western-style clothes such as jeans, perhaps even to eat meat, drink alcohol, and smoke (all frowned upon in Hinduism). They also want to be able to marry for love, irrespective of social and religious barriers, and to live apart from their parents.

▶ *These girls in Bangalore prefer to wear Western clothes rather than Indian clothes. On special occasions, though, they will dress in saris or salwar kameez.*

The New Consumers

The cities are home to India's "yuppies." These are the children whose parents have grown wealthy from the business boom since the 1990s. Both parents and children enjoy nothing better than a trip around the shops with their credit cards, in search of the latest European designer-label fashions or a state-of-the-art Japanese home-entertainment system. They like to eat out in expensive restaurants and to work out at health clubs. They like to read, write, and talk in English, and chat on their cellular phones.

Such behavior is very strange to many Indians, who have never had the money or time to buy luxuries and who have always been content with the traditional Indian way of life.

▶ *Bangalore by night. Nothing special to Westerners, perhaps, but it is for Indians, who are not used to seeing such a "light display."*

IN THEIR OWN WORDS

"I'm William Rikh and I work for an American credit-card company in Delhi. Ten years ago credit cards were almost unheard of in India. Very few shops accepted them to pay for purchases and even fewer people owned one. Only people who regularly traveled abroad had credit cards.

"However, there has been a revolution recently. Now there is a huge demand from businesses that want to be able to accept credit cards, and everyone wants to own a card—or even two! People have a lot more money to spend, thanks to all the new well-paying jobs in the computer and information technology industries. In five years' time I think that 75 percent of all adults in India will use a card when shopping."

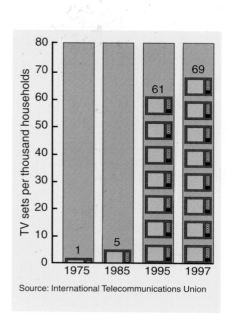

▲ *For these villagers in Rajasthan a road is for walking on, not for driving along. They are too poor to benefit greatly from the changes happening all around them.*

Village Life

Most wealthy city people look (and possibly feel) out of place in a village. For them, visiting a village is like stepping back in time. The men wear white dhotis, the women wear brightly colored saris. They talk in Hindi or a local language. There are no vehicles in the streets, except for a bullock cart or two. The shops stock only basic necessities. The homes do not have running water or indoor toilets and, often, they have no electricity.

▶ *The number of people who own a TV set has risen dramatically, but it is only a small proportion of the total population.*

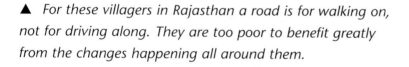

Source: International Telecommunications Union

In the villages, exercise means a backbreaking day in the fields, not an hour's jogging in a park. Food is precious and not something to be wasted. Villagers have no need of low-calorie meals or sugar-free drinks. Many of them do not have enough to eat. Being overweight is something to be proud of because it shows you can afford to eat well. Village life is tough, and it has changed little.

The Pull of the City

The widening gap between cities and villages is revealed in government statistics. They show, for example, that twice as many babies die in the villages as in the cities. Similarly, twice as many men can read and write in the cities as in the villages.

The prospect of better education and health facilities, along with higher-paying jobs, has attracted millions of villagers to the cities. The cities are now at a bursting point.

▼ *Farmers clearing fields in Rajasthan. Much of the work has to be done by hand.*

◀ *A woman weaving baskets in a poor district in Mumbai. Many city people have to survive on the little money they can earn from selling goods they have made themselves.*

Jobs and homes are in short supply, and hospitals and schools are full to capacity. As a result, new arrivals face disappointment and have to put up with living in shanty towns and working badly paying odd jobs.

IN THEIR OWN WORDS

"My name is Bhupinder (left, in the white shirt) and I live with my parents, my grandmother, and four brothers and sisters. You can see some of our neighbors in this photo, too! In India there are too many people and not enough homes. We are too poor to buy a house or apartment, so we have to rent a room from my father's boss. It's 9.8 feet (3 meters) wide and 13.1 feet (4 meters) long—a tight fit for seven people, but we manage.

"My mother cooks outside in the yard. There's also a hand-pump here for our water. Life is very hard for us. Every day I see how lucky other families are and hope and pray that I can get a good job so that I can look after my parents when they are old."

Changes at Work

8

In 1947 agriculture was the main business in India. The majority of workers relied on it for a job. It provided most of India's exports. The few industries built by the British were connected with agriculture, such as the factories to process freshly picked tea to make it ready for drinking.

Agriculture is still important, but less so than at Independence. It continues to employ the most workers, but its share of exports has dropped, and there are now many industries without any need of its products.

Industrialization

After Independence, India concentrated on setting up "heavy" industries, like iron and steel. India was lucky in having large supplies of coal and iron ore, so it did not need to import the raw materials.

The government took charge of all the key industries and planned their progress, telling them what they should do. A few private corporations were allowed in some parts of the economy.

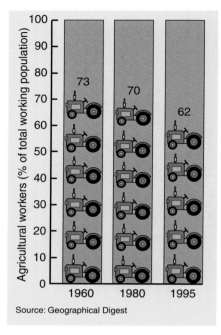

Source: Geographical Digest

▲ *The number of people working in agriculture is dropping steadily.*

IN THEIR OWN WORDS

"My name is Joaosinho do Rosario Vales. I'm a rice farmer in Goa. Hundreds of years ago the Portuguese ruled Goa and all of our names were changed into Portuguese. Goa has been part of India only since the 1960s, when the Portuguese left.

"I own four paddy fields, which produce about 270 pounds (100 kg) of rice each year. This is only enough to feed my family and I make my living by growing coconuts and mangoes and selling them in the market. I have two sons but only one of them helps me on the farm now—his brother has gone to work in a pizza restaurant in Saudi Arabia."

However, these corporations needed the government's permission to begin and a close eye was kept on what they did.

Industrialization was a great success. By the 1980s India had become one of the ten most-industrialized nations in the world. But government control was starting to do harm. Indian industries were modernizing more slowly than those in Europe and America, which had more freedom to do as they wished. India was short of consumer goods, too, such as TVs and fridges.

▲ *Workers at a stone quarry in Tamil Nadu. As more building work is carried out, the demand for stone increases.*

▼ *New factories are springing up on the outskirts of most towns and cities as a result of the expansion of business.*

Early in the 1990s the government accepted that it should step back from running the economy and leave more of it in the hands of private companies. It also realized that foreigners could play a vital part in India's next leap forward. They had the know-how to help update existing factories, as well as money to invest in new ones to make consumer goods. So the doors were opened to allow them in.

At the beginning of the 21st century, the partnership is a success story. New factories are opening every day. They are making everything from cars and potato chips to computers and washing machines. And thanks to the work they have helped to create, millions of people now have the money to afford them.

▼ *This map shows the location of India's major industries.*

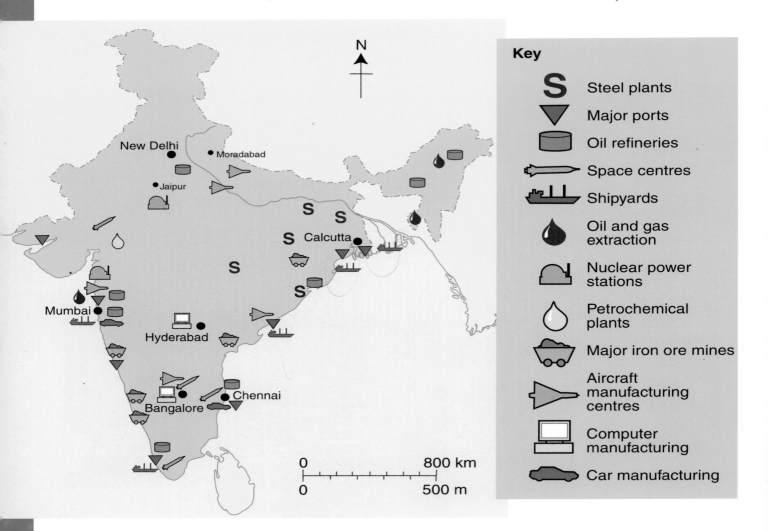

Key

S   Steel plants

▼   Major ports

⬭   Oil refineries

    Space centres

    Shipyards

◖   Oil and gas extraction

    Nuclear power stations

◌   Petrochemical plants

    Major iron ore mines

    Aircraft manufacturing centres

    Computer manufacturing

    Car manufacturing

Women at Work

In 2000, the United States' Ford Motor Company opened a car factory outside Chennai (formerly Madras). The locals were surprised when a lot of women were given jobs there. Ford said that it was looking for educated people who were willing to work hard. It did not matter whether they were male or female.

► *Women workers assembling TVs on a factory production line.*

IN THEIR OWN WORDS

"I'm Fay Singh. I'm a graduate of Chundigarh University. After I received my degree in English I decided to travel around the world for a few months. When I came back to Delhi I found a job making travel arrangements for business executives. Once it was assumed that women would stay at home and take care of the family—but no more! Many women now have careers. Look at me: I'm only 30 years old, yet I'm in a high-powered job. I work hard and am respected for it."

The attitude of the Ford Motor Company went against the way women are treated in India, where men have always been given priority. Women are still expected to stay at home and raise a family while men go out to work. New work practices are helping women to challenge these traditional roles. Now, many more have the opportunity to work, which gives them the power to stand up and speak for themselves.

▶ *A woman cooking chapatis for her husband. The age-old view of women only having a role in the home is under threat, especially in the cities.*

IN THEIR OWN WORDS

"My name is Dayakishen. Here I am, on the right, working with my father in his workshop. We cut up chopped-down trees and then sell the timber to carpenters. They make it into furniture, like chairs, benches, and beds. It's a very dusty and dirty job.

"I'm 15 now and I've been working here since I was 5 years old. I've never been to school. It was always work, work, work. Millions of children in India don't get the chance to go to school. Like me, they have to help their parents in their business. My brother is only six, but he's already hard at work alongside my father and me."

Working Children

One practice that foreign corporations have not been encouraging is the use of children as workers. India has the largest number of working children in the world. It is difficult to say exactly how many there are but estimates vary between 44 million and 100 million. Most of them belong to farming families, where children are expected to lend a hand, even if it prevents them from going to school. The remaining child workers have parents who are so poor that they need the extra money. Their children are often employed in dangerous jobs, like making fireworks, which adults would object to doing. They are treated badly and their health suffers. Laws ban children from working in many industries, but few employers pay attention to them.

▲ *These young children are helping around the home rather than going to school. They have been sent to get water for washing and drinking.*

The Electronic Revolution

All the business activity in India since the 1990s has sparked off an "Electronic Revolution." At work, computers have become a familiar sight in offices and factories. At home, people are using their computers to access the Internet. Computer studies are being taught in schools, colleges, and universities. Internet cafés are also springing up all over India.

Some people argue that computers are doing India more harm than good. They say that computers are replacing workers. However, supporters of the Electronic Revolution reply that computers boost business and lead to the creation of jobs.

▲ *Using an Internet café has become a part of everyday life for many city people.*

IN THEIR OWN WORDS

"My name is Bal Khattar. I joined the Indian Tourist Board two years ago. I was posted at Jaipur, where my job is to promote tourism in Rajasthan. I am able to do this more efficiently now because of the Internet. Computers, especially email, have revolutionized communications in India and I can even speak to travel agencies in the United States on my cellular phone from the center of the Thar Desert. Most middle-class families in Rajasthan have a telephone and a computer."

Service Industries

Computers have certainly helped to increase the number of jobs in the service industries—businesses such as banks, insurance companies, or travel companies. Service industries have grown rapidly in recent years. Banks, for example, have become busier as companies have prospered. As people have grown richer, they have begun spending more on savings, pensions, stocks, and shares. Both Indian and foreign firms have opened to advise them on how to look after their investments.

What Revolution?

However, the Electronic Revolution has not reached the countryside. Here, craftworkers continue to make things by hand in the way their grandparents did. The nearest they have come to a hi-tech revolution is to have a light bulb hanging from the ceiling of their workshop. This may seem extreme in comparison to the lifestyle in India's cities!

▼ *These metalworkers are using traditional tools and have no safety equipment. New business methods have not yet made an impact here.*

9

The Way Ahead

Today there are 17 million millionaires in India. As a group, their riches far, far exceed the combined wealth of all those who live below the poverty line. The poverty line is the minimum amount of money needed to eat properly: people with an income below it are considered to be poor. At the moment the line is drawn at about $3 per month. This means that 30 percent of India's population (around 300 million people) lives in poverty. The majority of these very poor people live in the countryside. (This is only a government estimate. The real figure is probably even bigger.)

Poverty does not only mean a lack of money. When you are poor you also lack many of the things you need for a decent life. Besides a lack of food, the poor do not have proper homes, or a nearby school, or hospital. All these can help them get out of poverty. Without them, it is very difficult, if not impossible, to escape from it.

▼ *Signs of the changes sweeping India can be found everywhere.*

Since the 1990s India's rich have grown richer, while the poor have remained poor. More new shops and clubs have been built for the rich than schools and hospitals have been built for the poor. The main task facing India now is to reverse this situation. It is not going to be easy, but India has the means to do it.

▶ *Old India is rapidly being forgotten by these young Bangaloreans, hanging out together at a city center café.*

IN THEIR OWN WORDS

"My name is Shaik Basha Ahmar. I'm 25 years old and I work for a company in Hyderabad that develops computer software for firms in the United States. Next year I'm going to work in California for five years. Over there I will earn ten times what I do here.

"People criticize me for joining the 'brain drain' out of India. 'All our best people are leaving,' they say. How can India progress without them? I reply that I will learn a lot about computers and business in America. This will benefit both me and India when I return. I have no plans to settle there. My roots are in India. This is my real home. I want to grow old here."

Glossary

Agriculture Farming the land.

Consumer Someone who buys or uses goods and services.

Cyclone A violent tropical storm.

Deforestation Cutting down too many trees in one area.

Dhoti A long piece of cloth, wound around the waist and then up between the legs, to look like baggy trousers.

Diversified Made a wider range of products.

Drought A long period when there is very little rain, or no rain at all.

Economy All the business activity in a country.

Electronic Revolution The great changes being brought about by the use of computers.

Emissions Substances released into the atmosphere.

Exports Goods that are sold to other countries.

GNP per capita GNP stands for Gross National Product, the total amount of money earned by all a country's businesses in a year. "Per capita" is Latin and means "per person." GNP per capita is the figure you get by dividing the total wealth produced by the total population.

Hydroelectric power The force of falling water used to generate electricity.

Import To bring goods in from abroad.

Independence When a country begins to rule itself, after being ruled by another one.

Industrialize To build many new industries.

Life expectancy How long people are expected to live.

Literate Being able to read and write.

Mineral A hard substance (e.g. coal) that can be dug out of the ground.

National Grid The system of cables that transport electricity around a country.

Peninsula A narrow strip of land jutting into the sea from the mainland.

Plateau A flat area of high land.

Refining Making something pure.

Reservoir A lake used to store water.

Salwar kameez A loose tunic and trousers.

Sari A long piece of cloth wrapped around the body and tucked into the waist.

Slums Areas of badly built, overcrowded housing.

Softwood Wood from cone-producing trees, e.g. pine.

Standard of living A measure of what your life is like. A "high" standard means you can afford all you need. If you cannot afford all you need, you have a "low" standard.

Statistics Information shown in the form of numbers.

Stocks and shares Two ways of loaning money to a business.

Subsistence farming Producing only enough food for the farmer's own needs, rather than producing food to sell.

Water cycle The natural movement of water in the environment, falling as rain, draining into rivers and seas, and then evaporating into the atmosphere.

Further Information

Books

Ganeri, Anita. *Journey Through India*. Topeka: Econo-Clad Books, 1999.

Ganeri, Anita. *What Do We Know About Hinduism?* New York: Peter Bedrick Books, 1996.

Goodwin, William. *India (Modern Nations of the World)*. San Diego: Lucent Books, 2000.

Kagda, Falaq. *India (Festivals of the World)*. Milwaukee: Gareth Stevens, 1997.

Kalman, Bobbie. *India: The Culture*. Topeka: Econo-Clad Books, 1999.

Marchant, Kerena and Rebecca Gryspeerdt. *Hindu Festivals*. New York: Raintree Steck-Vaughn, 2001.

Marchant, Kerena. *Hindu Cookbook: Holiday Cookbooks From Around The World*. New York: Raintree Steck-Vaughn, 2001.

Park, Ted. *Taking Your Camera to India*. New York: Raintree Steck-Vaughn, 2001.

Useful Addresses

Indian Museum-Calcutta
27 Jawarharlal Nehru Road
Calcutta 700013
India

The Government of India Tourist Office
1270 Avenue of the Americas
Suite 1808
New York, NY 10020

Websites

http://members.aol.com/Donnclass/
Indialife.html
Find out plenty of information about the three major time periods of ancient India. Also, you can learn about what kids did during that time period, what they wore, where they went to school, and more!

www.indolink.com/Kidz/main.html
Read stories and fables from India, play games, solve riddles, and more at this informative and fun web site.

www.wildlywise.com/wlf_index.htm
This web site lets you get an up-close look at some of India's wildlife, including tigers, spotted deer, and elephants.

www.wildlywise.com/rsvs_index.htm
Take a tour through some of India's most famous wildlife parks. Enjoy your visit!

Index

Page numbers in **bold** refer to photographs, maps or statistics panels.